Chief Joseph

History Maker Bios

Jane Sutcliffe

BARNES & NOBLE

NEW YORK

Illustrations by Tim Parlin

Text copyright © 2004 by Jane Sutcliffe
Illustrations copyright © 2004 by Lerner Publications Company

This 2006 edition published by Barnes & Noble Publishing, Inc.,
by arrangement with Lerner Publications Company, a division of
Lerner Publishing Group, Minneapolis, MN.

Barnes & Noble Publishing, Inc.
122 Fifth Avenue
New York, NY 10011

ISBN 0-7607-3914-5

Printed and bound in China

06 07 08 09 10 MCH 10 9 8 7 6 5 4 3 2

TABLE OF CONTENTS

INTRODUCTION

Chief Joseph was a leader and protector of the Nimipu or Nez Perce *(nez purss)* tribe of Native Americans. His people lived in the American Northwest for thousands of years. Then white settlers came. Government officials told Joseph that the Nez Perces would have to move. Joseph said no. He fought for the freedom of his people to keep their home.

Joseph did not want war. He tried to fight for his land with words and ideas. War came anyway. But Joseph's wisdom, courage, and dignity earned him the respect even of his enemies.

This is his story.

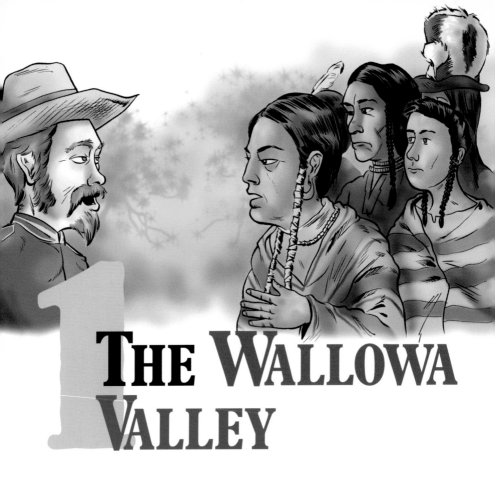

1 THE WALLOWA VALLEY

Joseph loved two things above all else.
First, he loved his people. They called themselves the Nimipu *(nee-mee-poo)*, which means "The Real People." White people called them the Nez Perce.

And he loved his home, the Wallowa Valley. The Wallowa was a handsome land of clear waters and tall mountains.

Someday the valley would be part of the state of Oregon. But when Joseph was born in 1840, it was still part of the Nez Perce homeland.

The Nez Perce were wanderers. They moved with the seasons to hunt, or fish, or gather wild plants. In each new place, they set up the animal skin tents, called tipis, that were their homes.

The Nez Perce loved the waving grasses and beautiful mountains of the Wallowa Valley.

Not all the Nez Perce lived in the Wallowa. Joseph's people lived in small groups called bands. Some bands lived as far away as present-day Idaho and Washington. Each band had its own chief.

Joseph's father, Tuekakas, was the chief of the Wallowa band. White people called Tuekakas "Old Joseph." His son was "Young Joseph."

In 1855, when Joseph was fifteen, he traveled with Tuekakas to an important meeting called a council. Chiefs from other bands were there too. The chiefs met with officials of the U.S. government.

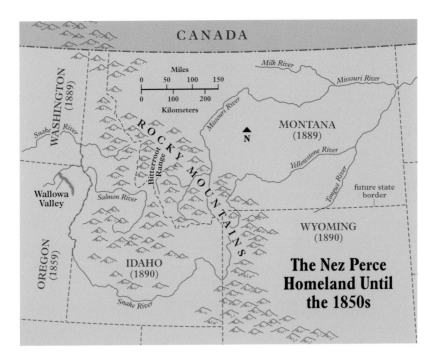

The officials explained that white settlers were coming. The settlers needed land to build houses and farms. The officials wanted the chiefs to give up some of their land for the settlers. The rest of their land would be set aside, or reserved, for the tribe. The officials promised that these reservations would be only for the tribe. No whites would be allowed there.

The Wallowa Valley was inside the reservation's borders. Tuekakas thought the plan was a good way to save his land for his children and their children. He signed the agreement, called a treaty.

Thousands of white settlers moved to the American Northwest in the 1800s.

For five years, life in the Wallowa went on as it always had. Then, in 1860, gold was found on Nez Perce land. Suddenly thousands of white miners rushed to the reservation, hoping to strike it rich.

The Nez Perce expected the U.S. government to make the miners leave. Instead, in 1863, officials held another council. They offered the Nez Perces a new—smaller—reservation in Idaho. The new reservation did not include the Wallowa Valley or most of the Nimipu homeland.

Some chiefs signed the new treaty anyway. Tuekakas and the others refused. They said that the government was stealing their land. They called the treaty a "thief treaty."

Tuekakas wanted to make sure everyone understood that the Wallowa belonged to his band. He planted poles all around the land. He told Joseph, "Inside is the home of my people—the white man may take the land outside."

Joseph's father, Tuekakas, refused to give up the Wallowa Valley.

Joseph was strong, tall, and handsome. But his mouth turned down at the corners, which made him look sad.

By this time, Tuekakas was an old man. The band chose Joseph to take his father's place as chief. It was a good choice. The band respected Joseph. He had grown into a gentle and wise young man.

As chief, Joseph looked after everyone in his band. He had a family to care for too. He was married to Springtime, the daughter of another chief. They had a little daughter named Sound of Running Feet.

One day, in 1871, Tuekakas sent for Joseph. He told Joseph that he was dying. "When I am gone, think of your country," Tuekakas said. "Always remember that your father never sold his country." Joseph promised that he would protect the Wallowa Valley, even with his life. He held his father's hand as Tuekakas died.

Joseph buried his father in the land they both loved. Would he be able to keep his promise?

SAY IT THIS WAY

French-Canadian fur trappers called the Nimipu the "Nez Percés" (nay pear-say). That is French for "pierced noses." The fur trappers noticed that some members of the tribe had pierced noses. They wore shells in their noses as jewelry.

Nose jewelry went out of fashion among the Nimipu. But the name stuck. In time Americans came along who pronounced the words differently. People still use their pronunciation: nez purss.

2 BROKEN BARGAIN

Joseph's first test as chief came at once. White cattle ranchers were moving into the Wallowa Valley. Joseph asked them to leave. The Wallowa belonged to the Nez Perce, he told them. The ranchers were puzzled. All they knew was that the U.S. government had bought the land. That was that.

So Joseph took his argument to the government. He reminded officials that his father had never signed the "thief treaty." He had never sold the Wallowa Valley.

It didn't matter, Joseph was told. Other chiefs had signed the treaty. Joseph's band no longer had any right to the Wallowa. They would have to go to the reservation in Idaho.

The U.S. government built a military post on Nez Perce land to try to keep whites and Nez Perces from fighting.

Joseph was stunned. How could the other chiefs give away what they did not own? Over and over, Joseph explained his case to government agents. Some of the officials were moved by Joseph's words. They suggested that the government allow the Nez Perce to stay in the valley. But in the end, the answer was always no.

In Joseph's Words

"Suppose a white man should come to me and say, 'Joseph, I like your horses, and I want to buy them.' I say to him, 'No, my horses suit me; I will not sell them.' Then he goes to my neighbor and says to him, 'Joseph has some good horses. I want to buy them, but he refuses to sell.' My neighbor answers, 'Pay me the money, and I will sell you Joseph's horses.' The white man returns to me and says, 'Joseph, I have bought your horses, and you must let me have them.' If we sold our lands to the Government, this is the way they were bought."

At first, General Howard called taking the Wallowa away from the Nez Perce a "great mistake."

Joseph felt helpless. By this time, he had spent years talking to the whites about his land. "It is strange they cannot understand me," he said.

Some of the young men in Joseph's band were tired of all the talk. They wanted to attack the whites and drive them out of the valley. But Joseph knew that would be foolish. "We were but few, while the white men were many," he said. "We were like deer. They were like grizzly bears."

In May 1877, Joseph met with General Oliver O. Howard. He was the U.S. Army commander in the Northwest. General Howard told Joseph that the time for talk was over. He threatened to send armed soldiers to force the Nez Perce out of the Wallowa.

The Nez Perce were expert horse breeders. They raised many kinds of horses, including the spotted Appaloosa.

Howard gave Joseph's band thirty days to move from the Wallowa Valley in Oregon to the reservation in Idaho. The band hurried to pack up everything they owned. Then they said good-bye to the valley they all loved.

By early June, the band reached a meeting place called Rocky Canyon. Other Nez Perce were there too. Joseph's band greeted friends and relatives from other bands. The get-together was part council, part fun. The Nez Perce were celebrating the last few days of their old way of life.

At first the gathering was peaceful. Then some of the warriors began to parade their horses. It is said that one young man named Shore Crossing was prancing his horse at the end of the parade. That was a place of honor for only the bravest warrior. His horse accidentally stepped on some food that had been left in front of a tipi. The tipi's owner shouted at Shore Crossing. "If you are so brave," he said, "why don't you go kill the white man who killed your father?"

The Nez Perce lived in tipis. Tipis were easy to move when the Nez Perce traveled.

Shore Crossing became wild with anger. "You will be sorry for your words," he snapped. He and two friends rode off. Other young warriors later joined them. For two days, the braves hunted down and killed white settlers. When they were finished, at least fourteen settlers were dead.

Joseph had tried so hard to avoid war! But it was too late. He knew that soon the soldiers would come.

3 THE NEZ PERCE WAR

The Nez Perce had to hide. Soldiers would be looking for them. The chiefs moved everyone to White Bird Canyon, about sixteen miles away. Then they waited.

The next morning, before dawn, one hundred U.S. soldiers made their way into the canyon. Six Nez Perce warriors met the soldiers. The warriors carried a white flag. This was a sign that they wanted peace. Maybe, in the dim light, the soldiers did not see the flag. Maybe the soldiers were just surprised. One of them fired two shots at the warriors.

One hundred soldiers and sixty warriors fought at White Bird Canyon.

The Nez Perces hoped to find safety in the buffalo country of Montana.

The Nez Perce had hoped for peace. But they were ready for war too. Warriors were hidden all around the canyon. They opened fire on the soldiers. The battle lasted only minutes. The panicked soldiers retreated. They left behind thirty-four dead. Four men were wounded. Only two Nez Perce were wounded.

Joseph and the other chiefs knew that many more soldiers would be coming. Their only hope was to stay out of the soldiers' reach. They decided they would go to "buffalo country"—Montana. Surely the Idaho soldiers would not follow them across the border.

Joseph helped everyone prepare for the long journey. Most of the 750 people in the tribe were women, children, and old people. Joseph was their guardian. He looked after the camp. He kept the people calm. Most of all, he tried to keep them out of danger. The other chiefs had experience in battle. They became the war chiefs of the group.

Joseph's brother Ollokot was a brave and fierce warrior. He was one of the band's war chiefs.

General Howard and his soldiers always seemed to be two days behind the Nez Perce. They called him "General Day After Tomorrow."

As the Nez Perce moved, General Howard and his men followed. The band had brought over two thousand horses with them. When one horse got tired, a rider switched to a fresh one. With so many horses, Joseph's people were usually able to stay ahead of the soldiers. They moved quickly over the rugged land.

Sometimes the soldiers caught up. Once, the Nez Perce were camped by the Clearwater River. Suddenly soldiers came from the woods. They surprised the warriors. Joseph rushed to help the women and children escape.

The Nez Perce needed to cross the dangerous Bitterroot Mountains to get to Montana.

The Nez Perce pushed on. Soon all that stood between them and Montana were the Bitterroot Mountains.

But what a barrier they were! The trail through the mountains was twisting and very steep. In some places, the Nez Perce had to make their way past dangerous cliffs. In others, they scrambled over large rocks and fallen trees.

It took Joseph's people nine days to pass through the mountains. Then they found a different kind of barrier. Where the trail passed through a narrow canyon, U.S. soldiers had cut down trees. They built a log barrier to stop the Nez Perce.

Joseph spoke to the soldiers. He told the men that his people were peaceful. Still, the soldiers refused to let them through. "You cannot get by us," a soldier boasted. Another chief replied, "We are going by you without fighting if you will let us, but we are going by you anyhow."

The next morning, the soldiers woke up to an amazing sight. The Nez Perces had ridden their horses high up the mountainside beside the trail. Joseph was leading them *around* the barricade.

The Nez Perce were in Montana! One man spoke for them all: "No more fighting!"

THE LEGEND OF CHIEF JOSEPH

Newspapers all over the country carried articles about the Nez Perce War. They wrote about Joseph the "war chief," who kept outsmarting the U.S. Army. Soon Chief Joseph was famous as a clever military leader. But reporters did not understand that Joseph's job was to protect the people. They thought he was leading the warriors into battle.

ATTACKED!

Early on the morning of August 9, the Nez Perce were asleep. A few women left their tipis to add wood to their families' fires. Then they went back to bed.

Suddenly, U.S. soldiers came charging into the camp. They fired their guns into the tipis. For a few moments, there was panic. Then Nez Perce warriors grabbed their guns and returned the fire. When they were hit, their wives picked up the guns and continued fighting. The Nez Perce drove the soldiers back.

A Nez Perce made this drawing of the early morning attack.

Joseph had hoped to find freedom and safety in Montana. But the soldiers' attack changed his mind.

The Nez Perce lost fifty women and children and thirty warriors that day. Springtime, Joseph's wife, was wounded. Years later, he remembered the attack with bitterness. "The Nez Perces never make war on women and children," Joseph said. "We would feel ashamed to do so cowardly an act."

Joseph's people lost more than friends and family. They lost their dream of freedom in Montana. How could they ever feel safe in the United States again? Instead, they headed for Canada.

Once again Joseph helped look after his people. This time, there were wounded to care for too. Even so, the Nez Perce stayed ahead of the soldiers.

By September 29, the Nez Perce had been on the run for fifty-one days. They had traveled one thousand miles. General Howard's army was far behind.

The chiefs called for the camp to stop near the Bear Paw Mountains, only forty miles from the Canadian border. That night, the Nez Perce rested by their fires. They didn't realize that another group of soldiers, led by Colonel Nelson Miles, was speeding toward the Bear Paw Mountains.

Colonel Nelson Miles once boasted, "I could clean this country entirely [of Native Americans] in four months."

The next morning, the Nez Perce took their time getting ready for the day's ride. Most of the horses were resting just outside the camp. Suddenly, a scout—a warrior keeping a lookout for the enemy—came racing toward the camp. He fired his gun and waved a blanket. That was a signal. It meant that enemies were about to attack!

Almost at once, the Nez Perce heard the roar of galloping hoofs. It was soldiers! Hundreds of them charged the camp.

Some of the families had already packed their horses. They managed to get away. The others had no chance. Soldiers had turned the rest of the horses loose. Without horses, there was no escape.

U.S. soldiers made a surprise attack on the Nez Perce.

Joseph fought with a Winchester
rifle much like this one.

Joseph and his daughter found
themselves surrounded by panicked horses.
Joseph tossed the girl a rope. He told her to
catch a horse and follow the people who
had escaped.

Joseph did not try to escape. Instead, he
dashed to his tipi to find his wife. When
Joseph reached his tipi, his wife handed
him his rifle saying, "Here's your gun.
Fight!"

Joseph did. All day and into the night,
Joseph and the warriors fought back. At
times he and the soldiers were not more
than twenty steps apart. Once, he saw six
warriors killed in one spot near him.

That night, the Nez Perce dug holes to hide in for protection. Snow fell as they dug. By dawn, five inches of snow covered the battlefield.

The next day, Colonel Miles sent a messenger. He had an offer for Joseph. He wanted the Nez Perce to surrender. In return, he promised, they would be allowed to go to the reservation in Idaho. That was, after all, where they had been heading when the war began.

Another chief, named White Bird, did not want to surrender. The soldiers might just kill them in revenge, he warned Joseph. He still wanted to try to slip away to Canada.

WHAT HAPPENED TO JOSEPH'S DAUGHTER?

Joseph's daughter, Sound of Running Feet, escaped from the Bear Paws battle. She and two hundred others made their way to Canada. Within a few years, though, she was homesick. She went back to the Idaho reservation to live. Sound of Running Feet never saw her father again.

Joseph could not stand to see his people suffer any longer. So he chose to surrender to Colonel Miles.

Joseph looked at his people shivering in their holes. They were starving. The children were crying. "For myself I do not care. It is for them I am going to surrender," he said.

At midday on October 5, Chief Joseph handed his gun to Colonel Miles. The words he spoke are still famous today: "Hear me, my chiefs! I am tired. My heart is sick and sad. From where the sun now stands I will fight no more forever." The war was over.

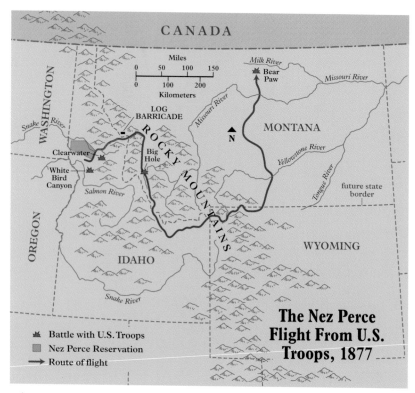

The Nez Perces' flight from U.S. troops lasted four months and covered 1,700 miles.

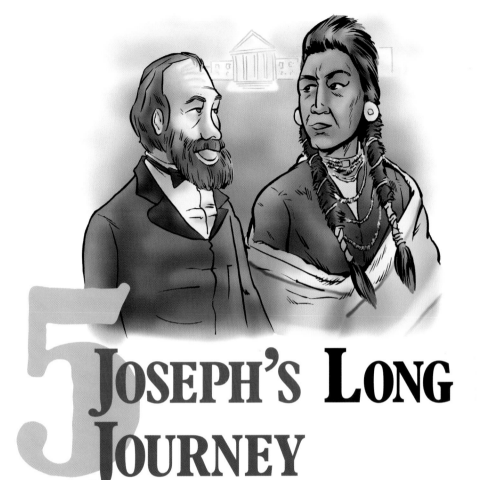

5 JOSEPH'S LONG JOURNEY

T he Nez Perce were exhausted and bleeding. They had lost 120 of their loved ones. They had lost their freedom. But they were going back to be with their people in Idaho. Colonel Miles had promised this.

Government officials had other ideas, though. Colonel Miles was ordered to send the Nez Perce to Fort Leavenworth in Kansas. There they would be held as prisoners. The colonel was unhappy that the government was making him break his word. He had come to respect Joseph. He even asked for permission to bring Joseph to Washington, D.C., to meet with government leaders. The answer was no.

After the war, the U.S. government sent the Nez Perce to Fort Leavenworth, Kansas.

U.S. officials invited Joseph to visit Washington, D.C., in 1879.

Life at the fort was horrid. There was no clean water to drink. Swarms of mosquitoes carried disease. By the following summer, twenty-one Nez Perces had died from illness. Many more were sick.

In July 1878, the government moved the Nez Perce again. They went to Quapaw Reservation in Oklahoma. Life there was no better. Within a few months, forty-seven more people were dead.

Even the government officials could see that the Nez Perce were in trouble. Some of the officials went to Quapaw. When they met Joseph, they were impressed by his concern for his people. They invited him to come to Washington, D.C.

Joseph met with President Rutherford B. Hayes twice in 1879. But Hayes did nothing to help the Nez Perce.

On January 14, 1879, Joseph gave a speech for officials in Washington. "My friends, I have been asked to show you my heart," he began. He told the story of his people. He spoke plainly about his struggle for justice. "The earth is the mother of all people, and all people should have equal rights upon it," he said. "I only ask of the Government to be treated as all other men are treated."

Joseph's speech was published in a magazine. People were moved by his words. This was not the "war chief" they had read about!

In June 1879, the Nez Perce were sent to a different reservation in Oklahoma. Life there was just as hard. By this time, many people were angry at how the Nez Perce were being treated. They sent letters and telegrams to Washington. Slowly, things began to happen.

In 1885, the Nez Perce were allowed to go home to the Northwest. Some of them went to the Nez Perce Reservation in Idaho, just as Colonel Miles had promised many years earlier. But many people were still afraid that Joseph would stir up trouble there. So he and his band went to the Colville Reservation in the state of Washington.

General Howard and Joseph met again in 1904. "Today I am glad to meet him . . . and be friends," Joseph said.

Life was better in Colville. The water was clean. There was plenty of game to hunt. But Joseph knew it was not his home. He could not forget his promise to his father. Joseph still hoped to return to the Wallowa Valley. Once, in 1889, the government offered to move his band to Idaho with the other Nez Perce. All Joseph had to do was give up any claim to the Wallowa. He refused.

LIVING WITH CHIEF JOSEPH

C. E. S. Wood worked for General Howard. After the war, Wood and Joseph became friends. Joseph invited Wood's twelve-year-old son, Erskine, to visit him at Colville. For months at a time, young Erskine lived in Joseph's tipi. Joseph taught the boy the old ways of the Nez Perce. Erskine said, "I can say truthfully, knowing him was the high spot of my entire life."